Dedication

To everyone
who has ever believed in me
and everyone
who is learning
how to believe in themselves.

The Moments That Freed Me

Laura Harrison

Copyright © 2020 Laura Harrison
All rights reserved.
ISBN: 9798642977965
Independently published

Contents

Part 1: The Girl I Used to Be

1. Falling for Strangers
2. Days When I Don't Want to Get Out of Bed
3. I Want to Feel
4. Scared
5. I Wish I Were A Bird
6. Take Me Away
7. Trapped in A Cage
8. Sunshine
9. Headphones On, World Off
10. Stuck in A Corner
11. Hidden Moon
12. Those Four Nights
13. A Week Without You
15. Tell Me Again
16. What I Hate
18. My Body Is My Home
19. You Look at Me
20. What Is Love?
21. If You Knew
22. Loved by You
23. I Live You
24. Freedom on A Page
25. Is This Real Life?
26. Love Like I've Never Known
27. What Would Happen?
28. Before I Forget
29. You Gave Me the Courage to Live
30. If You Leave
31. You Live in Me

32. Armour
33. Instruction Manual
34. We Love
35. This Is Not A Love Poem
36. Fade Out of View
37. The Truth Is...
38. An Explosion of Feelings
39. Let Me Fly
40. I Know How It Feels
41. Insanity
42. Don't Ask
43. Writer's Block
44. Something About You
45. Find A Way
46. Black and White
47. Words Unspoken
48. Make or Break
49. In Ten Years' Time
50. Fast Forward
51. So Much on My Plate
52. No New Notifications
53. Hands
54. Mountain
55. How Can We Live A Good Life?
56. Paradox
57. Someone to Call Mine
58. On the Sidelines
59. Glass Half Full
60. Two Sides
61. The Girl I Used to Be

Part 2: The Woman I Am Today

65. The Moments That Freed Me
66. I Went Outside
67. Alive
68. A New Sense of Perspective
69. Happiness
70. I Feel Like A Bird
71. Control
72. All I Knew
73. Remembering to Forget
74. Self-isolation Thoughts
75. Realisations
76. If I Died Tomorrow
77. Falling in Love with Life
78. Two Lives
79. I Laugh When I Think About You
80. Life After You
81. We Can't Hold on to People Forever
82. I Am Fat
83. I Used to Believe in Us
84. Now I Believe in Me
85. Love Is More
86. My Life Is A Rhythm
87. Me, Without You
88. A Better Person
89. A Life Worth Writing About
90. Dreams
91. No Longer Need You
92. Fuck It
93. Every Day Is A School Day
94. The Anchor and The Ship
95. Thinking About You
96. Wandering Soul
97. I Am Learning

98. Living on Borrowed Time
99. Single
100. The Life I Choose to Live
101. Cinematic
102. A Rare Occurrence
103. Butterflies
104. Life Is A Multitude of Choices
105. Remember How to Breathe
106. Clarity
107. Scavenger
108. Living the Ordinary Life
109. The Story of Us
110. Be Kind to Yourself
111. Reading Old Poems
112. It's All Uphill from Here
113. We Are Going to Die
114. Letting Go of Us
115. Hurdles
116. Narrator
117. Apologies
118. I Want to Be Good
119. New Years, Old Habits
120. On the Outside, Looking In
122. The Best Person
123. Jigsaw Puzzle
125. Everyone Needs Someone
126. Bloom
127. Would I Still Be Proud of Me?
128. The Woman I Am Today

130. Acknowledgements
131. About the Author

Part 1:
The Girl
I Used to Be

poems from 2012-2019

Falling for Strangers

I fall in love with every stranger I meet,
with anyone who shows
even the slightest interest in me.
I get caught up in their charismatic smile
and let myself get carried away
for a little while,
daydreaming of a fairytale romance
an unconditional love that will last
but then we go our separate ways
and I never see or hear from them again.

I fall in love with every stranger I meet
but what if no-one ever falls in love with me?

Days When I Don't Want to Get Out of Bed

Some days, I wake up in the morning
and something,
perhaps the torrential rain outside my window
or even the hurricane inside my head,
makes me want to stay in bed.
Sometimes, the world feels like a dartboard
and I am the target,
it feels like everyone is throwing sharp objects at me,
then pulling them out just to take another aim.
Most of the time, I feel like I don't belong here,
my own country feels foreign to me.
But my bed is my sanctuary,
no-one can harm me here,
well, no-one except me.

I need to remind myself of the temporariness of a day
just 24 hours and it will be over
and tomorrow could be the day everything changes,
the day I stop wasting my life away.
When I am alone, my mind works in overdrive,
running through thoughts that I can't override.
I need a distraction from these thoughts in my head,
so, I throw back the covers and get out of bed.

I Want to Feel

I want to feel beautiful and worthy
like all the places that I'll never visit.
I want to feel someone's arms wrapped around me
but they'd never reach me in this deep, dark pit.
I want to feel like I'm on cloud nine
instead of feeling like it's raining in my heart.
I want to feel the beauty of a rhyme
but I've forgotten how that even starts.
I want to feel the weight of the world on my shoulders,
because it's better than feeling nothing at all.
I want to feel happy and free,
oh, how I long to feel like anything but me.

Scared

My whole life is built up of fear;
I am so scared of dying,
yet terrified to keep on living,
not knowing where things go from here.

It scares me thinking about my future
and the fact that every day, it's getting closer.
I don't want to have responsibilities
or to grow up,
but if I don't, my life will go nowhere
and I'll always be stuck in this rut.

I am so scared of falling in love,
yet scared of walking this Earth alone.
How long will it take to find 'the one?'
How long will I be on my own?

But most of all I am afraid of change.
Maybe my life is fine this way.
It may not be perfect, but it's all I know.
What will I have when all I know goes?

I Wish I Were A Bird

I wish I were a bird so that I could be set free
from the repercussions of being me,
the memories of all the people who chose not to stay,
a future that is getting closer every day,
the disappointment of not being able to find work,
the realisation that life is no walk in the park.
I wish I were a bird so that I could be set free,
because life always tends to get on top of me.

Take Me Away

Take me away to a place
far away from here,
a place where I can disappear.
Where I can forget
everything that I've done,
everything that I've lost
and all that I've become.

Trapped in A Cage

I am trapped, like a bird in a cage
is anyone else on the same page?
I am tethered and my wings are broken
is anyone listening to the pleas I've spoken?

I am looking left and right, searching for an ally,
for the person who will never say goodbye.
People see me and people taunt,
to be treated as an equal is all I want.

Somewhere, there is someone just like me
trapped in a cage, waiting to be set free.
My fate awaits me, my destiny is near.
Until that moment comes, I shall stay here.

Sunshine

There's something about the way
the sun shines so brightly in the sky
that makes me fall in love with life
because if the wind and the rain
can't keep the sun hidden away,
then maybe my time to shine
will arrive one day.

Headphones On, World Off

Everywhere I go, it's the same old story;
people take one look and think that they know me.
They only see what's on the outside
and they don't mind telling me
that it's not what they like.
But when I put my headphones on,
I can't hear a word they're saying,
their ugly words can't faze me
because I never learnt how to lip-read.
Now I can dance to my own beat,
be the strong, confident woman
that I've always wanted to be.
And I don't care if anyone's watching,
let them stare, let them keep talking.
Because when my headphones are on,
the world is off,
so, it can hit me with every bullet that it's got.

Stuck in A Corner

I have a recurring nightmare that I'm stuck in a corner
and I just keep on getting smaller and smaller.
Now my nightmare has come true,
I am minuscule in a world that is huge.
My life is a puzzle piece that I can't make fit,
how long am I going to feel like this?

I want to be important and successful
but thinking about the future is so stressful.
No matter how much progress I make,
I just keep coming back full circle.
How long is it going to take
to get over all these obstacles?

I'll keep on trying to break down these walls
that I've put up around my heart.
I know that eventually I'll get through it all,
I know that eventually, my life will have to start.

Hidden Moon

Delicate whispers in the middle of the night,
I spilled my heart out to you as you held me tight.
You thought you knew me until today,
I'm like a moon, half hidden away.

My skin used to be a canvas for blood-red lines,
yet still you stayed when you saw the signs.
I thought I knew you, but I was wrong,
you really did care about me all along.

I feel invincible when we are together,
I just know our love will last forever.
Stars and sunsets may shine so bright
but you will always be my favourite light.

Those Four Nights

On those four nights,
I let my walls come down for you.
You got to know me better than anyone else
and I started to love every little thing you do.

On those four nights,
you held me in your arms until daylight came.
It made me feel as if I was safe from harm
and that's when I realised that my life had changed.

On those four nights,
you kissed me for the very first time.
All of a sudden, it felt like
everything wrong in my life would be alright.

On those four nights,
I lost my sister and best friend
but you were there for me all along,
you lifted me up and made me stay strong.

On those four nights
you changed my life for the better,
you were my flame when the light had died
and I'll love you forever.

A Week Without You

Day 1: I wake up, forgetting that you are no longer here. I look over at the bed beside mine, the bed that you not long ago occupied. I look around the room that we shared throughout our childhood, that we told stories in, gossiped in, argued in – but we knew that the latter would never matter because we swore that we would always be there for each other.

Day 2: Half of your things are still here, as if you are going to come back for them at any moment now. A part of me hopes for that. But what would happen next? Would you apologise for all the hurt you caused us? Would we all cry and hug each other and promise that nothing would ever come between us again? Or would you just come and go without a word as if you never played a huge part in my world? If I'm being honest with myself, I can't see you doing either.

Day 3: Mum insists that she puts up pictures of you around the house – as a sort of reminder that she has more than one daughter. I know that she is taking this the hardest out of all of us and I know that you are not bothered at all.

Day 4: I went on my first date today. It hurts knowing that I'll probably never get the chance to tell you about it, that you will never get to hear about any of my other first experiences, that I'll never have another conversation with you again.

Day 5: I'm trying to block out memories of you by listening to music but all my favourite songs are ones that we listened to together, reminding me of concerts we went to together, good times we had with each other. It's time to find some new music.

Day 6: All of your things and everything that reminded me of you are now gone – thrown away in a desperate attempt to forget it all – it didn't work. You are like a ghost, haunting my every thought.

Day 7: I sat down, and I wrote this poem. I can't decide whether to burn it or post it through your letterbox.

Tell Me Again

I have that red dress on,
the one that I wore when we first met
and my lips are painted crimson to match.
Yet I still don't have any confidence in me.
Tell me again that I'm pretty.

I'm crying again,
for the second time today
and I don't even know why.
All I know
is that you make everything better
when you say those three magical words.
Tell me again that you love me.

My mind is playing tricks on me,
telling me that we won't last,
that you'll get bored of me,
like a novelty that is no longer new.
Tell me again that you'll never leave.

I'm feeling worthless,
like I don't matter to anyone.
But you look at me,
like I put the stars in the sky.
Tell me again that I'm your everything.

What I Hate

One moment you were here,
the next you were gone
and even though I've known you my entire life,
it doesn't seem like that long.
I guess it just never occurred to me
that we had an expiry date,
but just like milk,
things between us eventually turned sour
and now the love I once had for you
has been replaced by hate.

I threw away everything that reminds me of you
in a mad frenzy to forget it all,
to pretend that you don't exist.
But I also forgot about my memories
because you are in every single one of them
and try as I might
they are the one thing that cannot be destroyed.
And I'm annoyed at myself
for taking you for granted,
for thinking that we would make many more memories.
Now I have to deal with the fact
that you are never coming back.

And I take back what I wrote before;
I could never hate you.
What I hate is that I can't hear your name
without reacting to it,
that I can't think about you
without missing you,
that so many of my memories
have been infested by you.
But most of all, I hate the fact

that I'm not writing about a lover,
but my sister,
because aren't family supposed to stick together?

My Body Is My Home

I used to stand in the mirror and pinch my skin,
tried to imagine what my life would be like
if I were thin.
Would it work?
Would there be no more cruel names?
Would I finally feel beautiful and brave?
I used to tell my body that it would never be worthy,
that no-one would ever love anything so ugly
but then, you came into my life
and you said until I believed,
that you'd found everything you had ever wanted, in me
and the way you caress my body,
the way that makes it hard to breathe,
makes it impossible to even think
that you'd be lying to me.
You love me, especially the parts of myself that I hate
but I am trying not to these days
because you made me realise that my body is my home,
so, it's about time that I started treating it like one.

You Look at Me

You look at me as if I put the stars in the sky
but please don't expect me to be extraordinary
I am nothing special, I'm just an ordinary person.
There are going to be days when I get mad or sad
or days when I can't even be bothered to get out of bed.

You look at me as if I am Cleopatra or Joan of Arc
but I am not a strong woman,
there are going to be times
when I'll shut myself off from the world,
when I'll build walls around my heart
and I won't want to see anyone, including you.

You look at me
and you see something about me that I can't see
but you never expect me to be something I can't ever be
and despite all these terrible traits
that I've listed about myself,
I know that you will always stay
because you look at me and I hear "I love you."

What is Love?

Love is a four-letter word,
one that is very rarely heard.
Love is gentle and kind,
it is never shallow, love is blind.
It's sharing your secrets with someone you can trust,
love is something much more than lust;
it's a deep connection to another soul
and finding the person who makes you feel whole.
Love is feeling safe in his embrace
and getting butterflies as he strokes your face.
It's the rush of pleasure as your bodies are entangled,
love is strong and can never be dismantled.
It's sharing your life with another
and wanting to be together forever.
Love is the thing that sets you free.
Love is, you and me.

If You Knew

Imagine if people had their entire lives
etched onto their skin,
a collage of all the things that they've seen
and the places that they've been.
Imagine if everyone's thoughts and feelings
were as clear as the glass
that some people's hearts feel as delicate as.
I hope that every person's life you have touched
was for the better
and that you weren't the reason someone's thoughts
turned bitter.
Because thoughts can be dangerous;
like a time-bomb that only has five seconds left
before it destructs
and thoughts can turn into actions.
I really hope that you aren't part of the reason
why someone's thoughts turned into actions.
Imagine if we knew what someone was going to do
before they actually did it.
Would you care?
Would you try to stop it?
Imagine if we didn't have to see the hurt
that we can cause someone
in order to know the right way to treat everyone.

Loved by You

They say don't expect anyone to love you
until you love yourself first
but, hell, you made me forget
that I'd hated myself at all.
And the first time you placed
gentle kisses on every inch of my body,
I suddenly realised
that I didn't care about any of my flaws.
And I remember those times
standing in front of the mirror,
wondering why someone
would make me this ugly,
wishing I could be someone other than me.
But you told me recently,
that the first time we met,
you were blown away by my beauty,
you told me that you
were so lucky to have me.
And whenever I'm with you,
you make me feel confident and strong,
I'm comfortable with all the parts of me
that I used to think were so wrong.
Even though I don't feel this way
all of the time,
at least I have you in my life
and even though I may never
love myself as much as I would like to
at least I know that I'll always be loved by you.

I Live You

You know all my secrets,
everything I've kept hidden inside,
all of my skeletons in the closet
and what keeps me awake at night.
You know what makes me happy,
and you know what makes me cry.
If there is ever a moment when I'm quiet,
you know the reason why.
But what you don't know about me,
the one thing that's most true
is that even though you are
the best thing that's happened to me
I do not love you.
Because 'love' is a word too inadequate
to describe the way I feel about you,
to explain everything that you've done for me
and everything that you've helped me through.
Every moment, I breathe you in,
as if you are the air that I need to survive
and in a way, you are
because I wasn't really living
before you came into my life.
So, in a way, I guess you could say
that I live you, like I've never lived before
because you've shown me what life is worth living for.

Freedom on A Page

I have so much that I need to say
but every time I try, no words escape.
I have lots of feelings that I want to share with you,
but my mouth might as well be sealed shut with glue.

But if you give me a pen,
my heart will start spilling onto the page,
through this black ink that I now control.
Give me a pen, and you will see my soul.

There are no boundaries when it comes to words,
I could create an entire new world
but I'd rather tell you about what I've been through,
about my life before I met you.
Read all about the hurt and pain,
give me a pen, and you will see,
freedom on a page.

Is This Real Life?

I wake up some nights with the feeling of dread
because I've had another nightmare
that you and I are just pretend
and I can't help but thinking
what if this is all just a dream?
What if I wake up one morning
and you aren't right there beside me?
What if I find out without warning
that you never even were?
The life that I lead now
just seems too good to be true
because I had nothing, before I met you
and I really hope that my mind hasn't made you up
and that you really are here with me
because for the past 2 years
you are the only thing that has made me happy.

Love Like I've Never Known

I couldn't survive if we ever did part
but a part of me wants to break your heart.
The only love I've ever known
is the kind that falls through,
so, I guess I just want to end things before you do.

Now that you are here, I couldn't imagine being alone
but being alone is all I've ever known.
I sometimes want to get back to the way I was before,
back when I had nothing to live for,
It may have been hell, but I knew what to expect.
Now with so many things changing I just have to guess.

But you keep me on the straight and narrow
and I'm glad that cupid shot us with an arrow.
We have a love better than any I've ever known,
so maybe it's best living life unknown.

What Would Happen?

I wonder what would happen
if we all said what we meant,
if we didn't worry about
thinking the same thoughts as everyone else
because our minds are half of
what makes us unique
and I find it fascinating
how we all strive to be ordinary
just in the hope of fitting in.

I wonder what would happen
if we didn't conform to society's rules,
if we just thought "Fuck it"
and stuck two fingers up
to the rest of the world.
Because what's the point of
over seven billion people being alive
if we all just act like we were put together
on an assembly line?

I wonder what would happen
if we suddenly decided
to be who we really are.
I wonder what would happen
if we just didn't care.
Probably nothing, probably everything
but wouldn't it be worth it
to not have to worry about
the pressures of being perfect?

Before I Forget

Once upon a time you were all that I had
you knew how to make me happy when I was sad.
I shared my worries and my secrets with you,
you were my sister and all that I knew.
You stayed my friend through thick and thin,
why did this have to change when you met him?

Now who is there to dry my tears?
Who can I count on to get rid of my fears?
Happiness is now just a distant feeling
and I no longer have anything to believe in
because you were always the person that I looked up to
and now that you're gone, I don't know what to do.

I try to kid myself that I don't miss you anymore
but truth be told, I just want my life back
to how it was before,
back to when you could always
make my problems seem smaller
back to when I actually had a sister.

A bunch of fading photographs is all that I have left of us
and some long-ago memories
that are crumbling into dust.
Now I am having trouble
remembering what you look like
and I'm finding it hard to be alright.
Give me a chance to see your face one more time,
before I forget every crease and line.
I want to share my life with you again,
before I forget what it feels like to have a friend.

You Gave Me the Courage to Live

I was living my life on autopilot, repeating each day like a broken record and hating every second of it.
But then you came along, like a miracle and everything changed. You made me do crazy things like go on dates and fall in love. You made me want to do something with my life like write poetry and share it with people. But most important of all, you made me realise that life is not there to be hated but lived and that's what you gave me the courage to do.

If You Leave

I lose everyone I allow myself to get close to
so, forgive me for sticking to you like cling film.
It's just that, I think my world would stop spinning
if I lost you too.
Because you are the reason why
I make myself get out of bed in the morning,
you are where my compass points when I lose my way
and no matter how upset I am,
you always find a way to make me smile.
How can I live without someone like you in my life?

I told you all of this once
when the sadness blanketed me again
and it all became too much.
I bared my heart and soul to you,
and unexpectedly, you held my hand through it all
and you promised me that you're not like the others,
you swore to me that you would never leave me.
But if you ever do,
please give me something better to remember you by
than something that brings tears to my eyes.

You Live in Me

You occupy my thoughts, my poems, my body.
You are what fills the silence when I am sad
the light creeping in through the darkness
and the dream that finds me in the middle of the night.
You are the shelter that protects me from the storm
and the one thing that's right,
when everything else is wrong.
You are my weakness, yet my greatest strength ever
and you show me heaven when I'm stuck in hell.
Yours is the smile that causes mine to appear,
you are everything that I hold dear.
You are the person who resides in my heart
and there isn't a surgeon who could tear us apart.

Armour

I think that I'm confident
but I still catch myself
judging my reflection in the mirror,
wondering if I'm enough,
wondering if I'm worthy of love.
I act like I don't care
about what anyone thinks of me,
I act like I don't need
anyone's approval
but deep down inside
I just feel so lonely.
So, I take my armour with me
everywhere I go
Because God forbid
if I bare my soul.
If my shield is up,
I'm protected from every weapon thrown
but the shield comes down
as soon as I'm alone.

Instruction Manual

I wish that life came with an instruction manual:
'Turn to page 52 to find out
how to forgive someone who set your heart on fire
and left you alone to put out the flames.'
Page 86 will explain, why sometimes
it feels like there's a brick wall in front of you,
stopping you from moving on with your life.
Yes, that's what I need, that would suit me fine
because I'm tired of all these obstacles,
tired of never getting anything right.
And maybe it could tell me
why I can't seem to hold down a job
or why I find it so difficult to figure out
whether or not I am happy.
Tell me, am I happy?
And if not, how do I get there?
When can I retire my mind and stop worrying
that I'm doing nothing with my life?
Tell me how to arrive
at that picturesque house at the seaside,
with everything I've ever wanted in my line of sight
and nothing in my mind except satisfaction.
I don't need lots of money,
material things are a waste of time,
I just want to grow old knowing
that at least I did something with my life.

We Love

We love like
deep conversations and late nights
and "I'm sorry, you were right's"
after bad fights.
We love like
Sunday morning, lazy days
and breakfast in bed,
perfectly content in your arms,
nothing needing to be said.
We love like
grandma and grandad
after fifty years of marriage,
telling stories about
how they survived it.
We love like
the ocean loves a wave,
no matter how many times
it's sent away.
Yes, we love,
despite our pasts and our mistakes,
our flaws and our heartaches.
Despite everything that we've been through,
we love like
two people should, in a generation
that has yet to learn how to.

This Is Not A Love Poem

This is not a love poem.
This is me after too many glasses of wine,
in the middle of the night when I'm feeling lonely
and desperate for someone to hold me.
This is not a love poem,
this is me being honest for once in my life.
I have a hard time admitting to my feelings,
I tend to keep them locked away at the back of my mind
where no-one can reach them.
But there's something about you
that has made me want to set them free
and I said I was being honest
so, here's a few things that I've never told you:
I love the way that you sing in the shower
when you think that I'm not listening
and I love that you're so weird
but you don't care about what anyone thinks of you.
I love that you still call me beautiful,
even though I've told you a million times that I'm not
and I love the fact that you put me before everyone else,
even when I give you every reason not to.
This is not a love poem,
but I **do** love you.

Fade Out of View

Even though we've been together
for almost three years now,
I still get surprised every time you kiss me,
every time you hold me,
every time you say, "I love you."
I guess I'm still getting used
to not being that lonely little girl
waiting for Prince Charming to come along.
I guess I'm still getting used
to the feel of you holding my hand
and brushing my tears away when I'm sad
because before I met you,
those are feelings that I'd never had.
And it all still feels like a dream,
too perfect to be true
and I'm scared that one of these days,
I'll wake up and you will fade out of view.
So, I'm capturing every memory of us
in my mind like a photograph,
all of the precious and beautiful moments
that we will ever have just in case you ever do.

The Truth Is...

It's been three years since I last saw you
and every time I tell someone I'm over you
I don't know whether I'm lying to myself or telling the truth.
The truth is,
I think about you all the time,
how could I not, with the number of poems
that I write about you
But I don't really get upset about it anymore
I don't spend my time looking at photographs of us
and staring out the door.
So maybe it's true that time does heal
but maybe it will take a little bit more
because the truth is,
I still miss you
but I think it's more of an ache for what should be here
because just like a tooth that has to be pulled out,
you were bad for me, I realise that now
but you were a part of my life for so long
I guess it was mandatory to miss
after you after you were gone.
Maybe I'm pining for the person that you used to be,
for the sister who I loved and grew up with,
not this person I no longer recognise.
And it's true that I don't know whether or not
this whole poem is a lie
because the truth is,
I haven't got a clue what I'm feeling,
but I just can't get you off my goddamn mind.

An Explosion of Feelings

Inside my chest there is a ticking bomb,
counting down the seconds until I finally explode,
until everything I've kept bottled up
comes rising to the top,
threatening to leave destruction in my wake,
but I've had so much practice over the years
that I know how to make it stop.

I try to be the strong one,
the pillar that holds everything up
but I always end up making myself feel down.
I know it's no-one's fault but mine
because I care about everyone, but sometimes,
even surrounded by a sea of people I know I am loved by
I still can't help but feel alone.

But I've always been a good girl,
I've mastered the art of keeping things hidden
at the very back of my mind
and I've gotten so good at it lately, that sometimes,
even I don't know the reason why I cry.

I've discovered that the mind works
in weird and sometimes, not so wonderful ways,
that really, each sunrise is just a reminder
that beautiful things occur every day.

And I've figured out that words
are so much better on paper than out of my mouth.
So, I shall allow the pen to be the metaphor for the bomb
in this particular poem,
because I prefer my explosions of feelings
to be written rather than spoken.

Let Me Fly

Treat my heart like butterfly wings,
be careful not to touch
because it is made of gossamer,
it could snap if I let you come closer.

Stare at me all you like
but don't catch me in your trap.
I want to be free to live my life,
falling in love was never part of the plan.

You can call me beautiful
but I won't change my mind,
like a butterfly,
I want to be free to fly.

I Know How It Feels

I know what it's like
to be trapped inside your mind,
to be a prisoner shackled to
the thoughts that you can't voice.

I know how it feels
to lose all self-control,
to forget how to make sense
of the world you've always known.

I know what it's like
to shut out the world,
to hide under your bed covers
where the demons can't emerge.

I know how it feels
to not know how to feel at all,
to learn how to fake a smile
and build indestructible walls.

Insanity

When the thing you fear the most
is not being in control,
what do you do when insanity
comes knocking on the door
to your soul?

Don't Ask

Don't ask me why I'm crying,
I don't even know,
it's just something that happens
every once in a while.

Don't ask me why I'm quiet,
I'm just in a mood,
I don't really feel like talking
if that's alright with you.

Don't ask me if I'm alright,
the answer will always be yes,
even when it feels like
a boulder is crushing my chest.

Don't ask me why I'm not myself,
I'm still figuring out who that is.
Sometimes, my mind just works overtime
and I don't know how to stop it.

Writer's Block

I'm wide awake at 2 AM
with a thousand words swirling around in my head.
I'm dying to get them down on paper
but I can't form a single sentence
when I pick up my pen.
This is writer's block at its worst,
when there's endless things that I need to say
but I can't express myself in my favourite way.
I guess my feelings will have to wait for another day
and now I'll try to get some sleep
if the incessant and indecipherable
words in my mind will let me.

Something About You

There's something about the way you say my name,
a delicate whisper that takes my breath away.
There's something about the way you kiss me
that makes me feel brave,
that makes me able to drive my fears away.
There's a certain kind of euphoria
when your body collides with mine,
an electrifying shock that shoots up my spine.

But there's that old familiar fear of hatred in me tonight,
the ones that tells me you never do anything right,
the one that pushes you away
when you try to hold me close
and tells you that I don't love you,
when I need you the most.
But just as I am about to walk out of the door,
there's something about you
that makes me fall into your arms once more.

Find A Way

Recently, I've been wondering if there is a future for us
because we seem to be stuck in one place
but I'll never give up on our love,
there is plenty of time for things to change.

We just keep going around in circles
and I keep being pushed to one side
but I know that we can jump these hurdles,
we just need to take it in our stride.

Even when the stakes are high,
I'll always be right by your side
and sometimes it's hard to stay on this slippery slope
but I am going to try
because nothing in life is ever perfect.
Things get broken, things get wrecked
but our love still exists despite these struggles,
and we are managing to overcome our obstacles.
Sometimes, it is so hard for me to stay
but I know that I'll find a way.

Black and White

Us poets, we're liars, all of us
we weave tales of happiness,
of love and hope.
When in real life, we're hanging by a thread,
desperately scrawling down hopeful words
to stop the mad ones in our heads.
We write about the world,
try to convince you that it's perfect
but even we don't have faith in these words yet.
Call it inspiring, call it wishful thinking,
call it whatever you like
but I want to believe in what I write.
I want to live my life out in the real world
and not just on paper,
I want to go outside and have adventures.
I want to smile, knowing that it's real
and I want to think that time does heal.
For once in my life, I'll try to trust my words
and believe that everything is going to be alright.
After all, it's right here in front of me in black and white.

Words Unspoken

There are a thousand words inside of me,
begging to be set free.
I want to tell my sister that I don't understand
why I no longer see her,
I want to tell my mother and father
that I don't think I can pretend to be happy
for much longer,
I want to tell you that I love you so much
but I can't see us together in the future.

These words want to be screamed out loud
but every time I open my mouth,
I don't make a sound.
It's like someone is grabbing me by the throat,
leaving me with no air,
forcing the words to stay where they are.

These words have been trapped forever
but when I sit down with a pen and paper,
they suddenly become brave;
they fly from my heart
and straight onto the page.
In just a moment, I experience freedom,
when I let go of the words so long unspoken.
But then I close my notebook
and the words get locked away,
never to be set free again.

Make or Break

Everyone says I'm the strong one
so why am I so weak when it comes to you?
Why can't I walk away
after everything that we've put each other through?
Because I think we both know
that this love has ran its course,
I guess I'm still just trying to pretend
that there's still time for us to be more;
I guess I'm just waiting for the clocks to turn back,
back to the way we were before.
You know that arguing about this
never gets us anywhere,
you know we can't carry on this way
because it's just not fair.
I don't know why I always set myself up
for these disappointments,
I don't know why I even bother
trying to clean this mess.
So, it's make or break this time, for sure,
if you keep on shutting me out,
then I'm going to have to shut the door.

In Ten Years' Time

I often wonder what I'll be like
in ten years' time.
Will I finally have my life together
or will I still be afraid of taking chances,
just waiting for things to get better?

Some people believe
that you can't change who you are
but I don't even know who that is.
Is this just a phase I'm going through
or am I destined to be stuck like this?

I always wanted to make something of myself,
to be the best that I could possibly be
but now I just want to find myself.
In ten years' time,
I want to be the real me.

Fast Forward

'Everything happens for a reason,'
but sometimes, I wish I knew what that reason was;
I wish I had a how-to book on life
because I'm tired of having to improvise
and never getting anything right;
I'm tired of having to be the strong one all the time.
I know that it's all a part of being human,
that life can't be perfect each and every moment.
but I wish I could just fast forward to the day
that my life starts getting better,
to the day that I start seeing in colour,
to the day that I get all of the answers.

So Much on My Plate

There's so much on my plate
that I've lost my appetite for,
because all I want
is the taste of your love
but that's not on the menu anymore.

No New Notifications

Silence is the loudest noise
when you're waiting for someone to text you goodnight
and you're so tired but you're wide awake
because you don't want to miss anything
while you're asleep
so, you lay awake, listening for the beep of your phone
wondering when the fuck you began to feel so alone.
Eventually, you slip into unconsciousness
but your thoughts follow
and you find yourself dreaming about
the possibilities of tomorrow.

Hands

I can't stop looking at my hands, at the whorls and lines engraved in them. I wonder how our lives can be mapped out in those lines before we even have a chance to start living. So maybe there is another higher power out there, deciding what is destined to happen to us. And I envy all the palm readers in the world, because if I could predict my future just by inspecting my hands, maybe I would have made better decisions and far less mistakes.

Mountain

Do you ever get the feeling
that everyone is growing up
and leaving you behind,
that everyone knows what they're doing
and you're still trying to figure out life?

Do you ever feel like
you're in a race against time
but no matter how fast you run,
you're still nowhere near the finish line?
Because sometimes it feels like
I'm in an elevator that only goes down,
sometimes it feels like I'm lost and will never be found.

But I'll never give up,
like a dog chasing its tail
because I believe that hope will prevail.
So, I'll keep on climbing this mountain
with all my fears strapped onto my back
and I won't look behind me
until I've finally reached the top.

How Can We Live A Good Life?

How can we be
surrounded by people all the time
yet still feel so alone in life?
Wandering around, looking for a purpose,
the pot of gold at the end of the rainbow
that will make all this worth it.

How can we spend
the better part of our life with someone
for them to end up as a stranger again?
Just another face that you see in your dreams
but your life with them
becomes nothing more than a distant memory.

How can we be
so alike, yet so different?
Different experiences and personalities
but the same worries and emotions.
Most people aren't as intricate as we may expect
so, I don't want to be afraid
of making connections with them
and I know that it can be daunting
to throw all our cards on the table and place bets
but I don't want to be afraid of truly living life
when it's the only one that we get.

Paradox

Some days I look in the mirror
completely bare-faced
and think to myself that I'm beautiful
but other days I catch a glance
and have to look away.

Some days I want to stay
burrowed in my bedsheets
but other days I want to escape
to anywhere other than here,
and be wild and free.

Some days I tell myself
that I need to grow up
but other days I'm perfectly happy
with staying innocent and young.

Some days I'm deliriously happy
and excited for what's ahead
but other days I'm frightfully sad
and can't wait for the world to end.

I'm just a girl
who doesn't know what she wants.
I'm a paradox
and I can't stop these conflicting thoughts.

Someone to Call Mine

Recently I've been keeping myself busy
just to waste the hours I'd normally spend with you,
we never did anything special
but it's the life that I was used to
and now I'm stuck, back in my old ways,
daydreaming of having someone
to kiss my worries away
but how can you come back
if you weren't the one to leave,
how do I remind myself that you're not what I need
when I always thought that you
were my happily ever after
rather than just a beautiful disaster.
How can I miss you
when I haven't loved for the longest time;
do I just miss the idea
of having someone to call mine?
Am I still scared of starting something new
or do I just miss how it felt when you said, "I love you?"

On the Sidelines

I want to be a friend to everyone I meet
because I remember a time when no-one
wanted to be friends with me
and I still get surprised when people are nice,
I'm still waiting for them to say it was just a joke,
I'm still waiting for the punchline.
Because I used to spend so much time alone
that I never thought I was the kind of person
people would want to get to know,
I never thought that just being me
would ever be enough.
Even though now I'm the life of the party
I still remember how it feels
to be on the outside looking in
at everyone else having a better life than me.
Even though I'm older now and I realise
that I'm not the only one who has ever felt like this,
I still wonder what it would have been like
to not grow up sitting on the sidelines.

Glass Half Full

Why do we remember the mean comments off strangers
more than the compliments?
Why do we forget times we were rewarded
but recall the punishments?
Why can't we laugh at a joke that's been told
over and over
but we can still cry at something
that hasn't happened in forever?
Why is it harder to feel happiness
than it is to feel pain?
Why do our minds do this to us
over and over again?
Why do we obsess over the things we can't control?
Because all we end up doing
is torturing our soul.

I know that there is beauty in this world
and I'm trying to be a glass half full kind of girl
if we were able to focus on the positive things in life
I really do believe
that everything would be alright.

Two Sides

They say there are two sides to every story
I wonder if I've been painted as the villain in yours,
if I've been added to the list of ex-lovers
who ended up doing you wrong.
I try to act like I don't care what you say
but who am I kidding when you were once
the best part of my day.
It feels strange that you're no longer in my life
when I used to believe,
that one day I would be your wife
and even though I pulled the plug on this disaster,
I always had hope that our story
would end with the words 'happily ever after.'
If I could be a fly on the wall,
would I see that you still love me
or that you have finally moved on?
If I could see your life without me,
I don't know what I would wish for.

The Girl I Used to Be

I never used to think there would come a day
when I would want to walk away.
I never thought there would be a time
when I threw away all the memories,
the souvenirs of an era when you were mine.
Now it's like you were never once a part of my life.
I used to believe that being loved by you
was my one-way ticket to happiness
but I guess I forgot that you have to love yourself first.
Because it's so easy for me
to get lost in my old thoughts again,
reminiscing about high school days
when I had no confidence or friends.
It's so easy for me to forget
that I'm no longer the girl I used to be
because I still feel so alone,
still cry at night, stuck in my childhood room,
the décor has changed countless times
but everything else feels the same;
same body, same heart, same stupid fucking brain.
Even though so much time has passed
and my life is no longer the same as the past,
I still take a trip down memory lane
and visit that girl who always felt useless and ashamed.
But if I could actually go back in time
and talk to the 17-year-old me, I would tell her that
the life she has isn't the life she's always going to live.

Part 2:
The Woman
I Am Today

poems from 2019-2020

The Moments That Freed Me

It's been said
that everything which happens in life
happens for a reason
and I'm no closer to figuring out why
certain things are in my past,
but I know that I wouldn't change them
if it was possible to go back.
So, I guess that time
really does heal all wounds,
and I guess that life
never throws anything at you
that you can't carry.
And sometimes I almost stumbled
from the weight of it all
but hope was always there,
ready to break my fall.
Now I'm finally happy
with where I am in life,
even though I know that eventually
it will change again.
But that's okay
because everything in life
is bittersweet,
not a single moment lasts for an eternity
but when all is said and all is done,
the moments that matter
are the ones that freed me.

I Went Outside

I went outside;
watched the trees gently swaying
in the summer breeze
as if dancing to a song
I could not hear,
allowed the sun to shine on me
and bless me with its radiance.
The birds were starting the day
with their cheerful chirrup
and I gladly hummed along.
I bade good morning
to the citizens of the world;
exchanged smiles and a "How do you do?"
I took a sniff of some pretty daisies
lying in a flower bed
and admired the spectacular colours
in the sky above my head.
I wondered why
I had ever despised my life
because I went outside
and fell in love with the world.

Alive

I find it fascinating how the passing of time
can make a door open on something
that you once felt you couldn't escape from,
how it can make you figure out how to become
the person you've always wanted to be.
It's amazing how people can do anything
they've ever wanted to do,
how they can break free from the shackles
that they've chained themselves to.
I used to live my life on autopilot,
each day just fading into the last.
I used to think that life was just about surviving,
until the day that I set myself free.
Now, I feel more alive than I've ever been.

A New Sense of Perspective

We should cherish the bad moments that occur in life
as much as the good ones
because everything is a lesson to be learnt,
every moment that we live through
defines us as a person
and we can't erase the things
that we're too sad to remember
because then there would be pieces of us missing
and to want a life filled with only sunshine and roses
is just wishful thinking.

I know we feel like we need to be happy all the time
but sadness and hurt need to be felt
in order for us to understand life.
Sometimes the pot at the end of the rainbow
is just filled with shit
but it's down to us to decide how we get clean from it.
We can give up on trying, and wallow in self-pity,
or, we can gain a new sense of perspective
and realise, that while life isn't always pretty,
if flowers can have the strength
to be resurrected every year,
then we can face all those memories that we fear.

Happiness

If we got everything we had always wanted in life
would we finally be happy
or is happiness nothing more than a notion
that is meant to be felt for no longer
than the split second of a moment?
Because I've always known it to be over so sudden
like an old friend you only see once every so often.
Do we even know what happiness looks like
or are we just aimlessly wandering around
hoping to stumble upon something
that makes us feel alive?
And are we doing what we genuinely want
or do we just feel forced to achieve
what everyone else has already done?
I want to believe that it's worth it
to feel every ounce of happiness before it's gone
and I want to believe
that it will always be found again.

I Feel Like A Bird

All the things that I used to think I wanted
were never the things that were right for me
and I'm so glad that I never actually got them
because I don't think I would now be the person
I've always wanted to be.
It's hard not to think about what could have been
but I'm in love with my life now
and I wouldn't change a thing.
This is a brand-new feeling for me
because I've never been satisfied,
until now, I've never been happy with my life.
I feel like a bird who's finally learnt how to fly
and I never want to leave the sky.

Control

I'm trying to learn
that we can't control other people,
how they think, how they feel,
how they act and how they treat us.
We can't even begin to understand
why some people are the way they are,
why some people carry invisible weapons
and leave us with emotional scars;
all that we can control is ourselves
and how we choose
to care for and lick our wounds.
We can choose to help others up
and listen to the voices
of those who just want to be heard
and we can choose to be
the best person possible
in this cruel and cunning world
and have hope that
that will be enough
to inspire someone else to pay it forward.

All I Knew

It's strange to think
that after everything we've been through,
one day I won't notice you in a crowded room.
There will soon come a time
when I'll forget the warmth of your arms
and the feel of your lips on mine
but what's even stranger
is the realisation that I don't want to remember
because when we were together,
I felt trapped under your spell
and I had to lose you to find myself.
I used to believe
that it would be impossible to survive
without you by my side
because for the longest time,
you were all I knew
but now that I've had a taste of freedom,
I could never go back to you.

Remembering to Forget

I found out today
that you have moved on
and I don't know what to do
with that information.
I'm happy for you,
I guess.
I just hope she knows
what she's got herself into.
I can't help thinking about
everything that we used to do
and the way you looked at me
like I was the only person in the room.
Now I guess
that you look at her that way too,
I guess you take her to the places
that used to belong to me and you.
But I had moved on
before I even left
so, I can't begrudge you for doing the same,
it just feels strange
that you have found someone else
who could one day want your name.
But I wanted the life that I'm heading towards
and I still do,
I just have to keep remembering to forget
about the one that I had with you.

Self-isolation Thoughts

I am comfortable with my own company
but sometimes I feel so lonely;
sometimes I get caught up in my thoughts,
in my low self-esteem and the feeling
that I'll die alone because no-one will ever want me.
I have friends that I'm so thankful to have in my life,
who I know will always be there for me
when I'm not alright
but it's easy to tell myself that one day they'll disappear
when they're not always physically here,
it's easy to think that they don't really care
and that I don't actually mean anything to them.
But then, someone will message me to ask how I am
or someone will say
that something reminded them of me the other day
and I'll remember how fortunate I am
for the life that I have and the company I keep,
I'll remember that there are people who care about me
and if, one day, fate was to intervene
and force us to part ways
I'll try not to be sad that they're no longer in my life
because I'll still have the memories
of when they were always by my side.
It's true that nothing in life ever lasts,
so, I'm going to appreciate the people in mine
until they end up in my past.

Realisations

I'm still realising that what I want and what I need
aren't always the same thing.
The heart wants what it wants
but life gives what you deserve,
I'm still realising that I don't know my own worth.

I'm still realising that I won't be liked by everyone
but that doesn't always mean
that I've done something wrong
because everyone has their own problems
and their own scars to heal.
I'm still realising that happiness
isn't found within other people.

I'm still realising that life doesn't walk in a straight line
because there are times when I trip and fall
and end up back in my darkest thoughts
and I'm still realising that for as long as I'm alive
I can always make it back out in time.

If I Died Tomorrow

I don't believe in God
but I want to believe that there's something
out there, bigger than us.
And if I were to die tomorrow,
I know that I would leave this world knowing
that I lived a life that was good.

Falling in Love with Life

I've always been alright
with the simple things in life,
I've always been fine
with staying inside.
But I've spent the last seven years
in the same place
so now I want to see the world every day.
I want to feel the warm sunshine
on my face
in a foreign city
where I want to stay.
I want to read more books
and write more poems,
listen to more music
that makes me feel something.
I want to create unforgettable memories
and discover everything possible,
I want to understand the world
and to be unstoppable.
I want to feel more joy
than my heart can contain
but most of all,
I want to fall in love with life
again, and again.

Two Lives

When you were a part of my life,
it was split into two;
the life that I loved
and the one that I had with you.
Because pretending that you made me happy
turned into a chore,
something that I had to do
to keep up the pretense
that you were all I was living for.
I realised after the first few years
that I only thought I loved you
because you listened when I confided in you
after I'd had a few beers.
But then I started to get my life back on track
and you were still stuck in the pit stop.
I guess I felt guilty for thinking of leaving
because I once believed that you
gave me the courage to keep breathing.
But now I know that I am the heroine
of my own story
and I no longer feel like I owe you something.
My life is in a good place now
because of choices that I made,
and I realised that I shouldn't fixate on a time
when I thought that you deserved a place in my life.

I Laugh When I Think About You

I laugh to myself now, whenever I think about
the way I used to feel about you;
like you were the part of me that was the best,
and that if I didn't have you, I'd have been lost.
Now I can't even remember
what I thought that I would miss
because I've never been happier than this.
And now, my life is finally just mine;
I can listen to music that you wouldn't have liked,
read my books without getting distracted,
and do everything that you never wanted.
I can live my life the way I've always wanted to
without feeling guilty for not thinking about you.

Life After You

I've discovered so many things in life after you
from music that makes me feel alive
to places I could see myself moving to
and I've accomplished so much,
things I never believed that I was capable of,
I'd convinced myself that I wasn't strong enough
to do anything without your love.
But life doesn't wait around, and time never pauses,
I realised that if I wanted to actually live
then I had to do something about it.
So, I dried the tears that became a permanent fixture
from all the years that I'd spent and wasted
trying to fix you.
I realised that I can't sacrifice my health
trying to heal people who don't want to be helped
and so, I took the plunge, took control of the situation,
I reminded myself that my life was mine
and that I didn't need you in it
for incredible things to happen.

I've discovered so many things in life after you
but my favourite out of all of them,
the one that makes me feel most overwhelmed,
is myself.

We Can't Hold on to People Forever

In life, people come and then they go
and sometimes all we can do
is hold open the door and let them walk through,
because we can't hold on to people
who no longer want to be held
we can't fix something that doesn't need to be repaired.
Sometimes in life, we're the ones to leave,
sometimes the person we want
is no longer the person we need.
The world keeps spinning and our lives carry on
without that someone who was in it for so long.
It's true that we can't rely on others to make us happy
because we're the only person who's writing our story.

In life, people come and then they go
regardless of that, we're never alone.

I Am Fat

I am fat.
I know this because
I see it in the mirror.
But I no longer obsess over it
and wish that I were thinner.
I am fat
but I am so much more,
I'm the poetry that I write
and the paths that I've walked.
I'm a beautiful mind
and the battles that I've fought.
I am fat
but that doesn't define me.
I am fat
but I am happy.

I Used to Believe in Us

I used to believe that you were my everything
but now whenever I think about you,
I feel nothing.
It's funny how time passes
and how quickly you can change your mind
about someone who was once
the best part of your life.

I used to believe that we would grow old together
but now whenever I recall moments spent with you
I realise that
we were never right for each other.
It's funny how easily you can move on
and how you can outgrow that person
you always believed to be 'the one'.

I used to believe that without you,
my life would never be the same
and it turns out that I was right,
it's so much better than it's ever been.

Now I Believe in Me

I used to believe that I was complete
because I had you,
that I didn't need anything else
in my life
just as long as you were mine.
But I had an epiphany,
a lightbulb moment
that life is so much more than just
having someone to hold and to talk to.
It took me a while to realise
that I didn't need you,
because I'd already left you once before,
I guess I just wasn't ready to give up
what I thought that I was living for.
I used to believe that there's a time limit
on changing my life,
but I've since realised
that as long as I'm alive,
it's never too late to make things right,
it's never too late to listen to the Universe
trying to guide me towards a better life.
So, as I walked away for the final time,
I realised that I didn't even want to look behind me,
because, from that moment on,
my future was all that I believed in.

Love Is More

Love is more
than just stolen kisses on a moonlit night
or a romantic dinner over candlelight.
Love is more
than tentative smiles when you first meet
or holding hands as you walk down the street.
Love is more
than secrets whispered in the dark
or saying those three words
after every heart to heart.
While it's true that it can't be seen,
love is so much more
than just a feeling.
It's a lifelong commitment,
it's acting upon plans,
love is more
than whatever it was that we had.

My Life Is A Rhythm

Confidence is a funny emotion
when you've always kept hidden,
when you've always hated attracting attention.
But now I can wear pretty dresses
with short sleeves
and not feel like everyone is judging me.
I can eat in front of people
and it's no big deal,
existing is no longer an act
that I feel the need to conceal.
And I've never been good at dancing,
but now my life is a rhythm that I'm moving to
and I don't care if anyone's watching,
I'll let them know just how much fun I'm having.

Me, Without You

I used to think that you
gave me the confidence
and ambition to live freely.
Now, ten months without you
I realise it was all me.
I guess seven years with you
broke the spell
and reminded me of the person
that I'm destined to be
because I'm more in love with life now
than I ever was with you
and I can't wait
for the next adventure I pursue.
It's like I lifted an anchor
that set me free
when I finally set sail to leave.
Now I'm writing something
I never thought would be true:
I love me, without you.

A Better Person

I hate making mistakes
but I'm learning to remind myself
that it's okay
and I know that I'm not perfect
but I'm learning to forgive myself
for trying to be.
I'm learning how to be
a better person to me.

A Life Worth Writing About

I feel like a lot of people
are scared of life changing
and I used to be the same
because it's so easy to get used to
the way things have always been.
But when we watch a movie
or read a book,
we are excited for what's to come,
for the plot twist that we don't see coming,
for the way we're left speechless at the ending.
I want to live the kind of life
that I would love to read about
because what's the point of being blessed with one
if you're just singing someone else's song?
What's the use of a life
where nothing changes at all?
If it's true what they say
and we see our lives flash before our eyes
right before we're about to die,
then I'm going to make damn sure
that I live a life worth writing about.

Dreams

Recently, I've been seeing you in my dreams
and you're always a better person than you are in reality.
You do and say everything just right,
you've got a job and that car
you always said you were saving up to buy.
In my dreams, we have the life
I used to think we would one day live
and you put in all the time and effort
you used to promise you were going to give.
In my dreams, I'm in love with you
like I never was when you were mine
and when I wake up
I'm glad that we're no longer together
because you could never be anything like dream you
in real life.

No Longer Need You

I always thought that I'd be broken if I didn't have you
always thought that I'd forget the melody
if we weren't playing the same tune
but it's funny how time can change your mind
because I no longer feel like I need you
like the stars need a night sky to shine.
I no longer feel like I need you by my side
in order for me to love my life.

Fuck It

In less than a year, I've done things
that I never thought I would do
like publish a book and finally leave you.
I used to be so scared of doing what I wanted
because I believed that the consequences
would be too daunting.
But now, whenever I overthink about things
that may not go my way
I just think, "Fuck it" and do it anyway.
It's my new mantra, my motto in life
and as long as I say it, everything will be alright.

Every Day Is A School Day

I'm getting better at being brave
in a world where I've always hidden away.
I'm trying to live each day as if it's my last,
making up for opportunities I've let slip pass.

I'm realising that it's okay to make mistakes
and that not all of them are able to be changed.
I'm beginning to understand that I'm only human
and that it's impossible to achieve perfection.

I'm learning how to let go of my living ghosts
and everything that I used to know.
I've figured out that the past must die
to give the present a chance to shine.

Every day is a school day
and I never want to put my books away.
If life is just a long exam,
I want to score as many points as I can.

The Anchor and The Ship

You were the anchor
and I am the ship.
Now I'm setting sail
and leaving you behind me;
I'm no longer afraid
of being set free
because when I was with you,
I never felt grounded,
but tied down to a life
that I never really wanted.
I've got a long journey ahead of me
but I can finally see the way
and I'm headed for places
I've always wanted to be.

Thinking About You

I think about you all the time
but I don't miss you,
missing you would be crying over all that we had
and running to your place,
begging you to take me back.
Instead, I'm living my best life,
creating memories that are just mine.
I'm doing things that you wouldn't have liked
and it doesn't even feel strange
that you're not right by my side
because I've realised that all you are
is a chapter in my life
that I've turned the page on.
You're just someone else
for me to write poems about,
another person I've learnt to live without.
And I got used to missing you
while we were still together
because I always knew
that I couldn't pretend to love you forever.

I think about you all the time
but I don't miss you
I guess I'm just reminding myself
of the life that I never want to return to.

Wandering Soul

I'm in a strange city
all by myself
and I've never felt
more at home
anywhere else.
I guess I'm a wandering soul,
deep inside,
a free spirit
that just needs room to fly.

I'm in a strange city
all by myself
and I've never felt
so alive,
I could happily stay here
for the rest of my life.

I Am Learning

This year, I am learning.
I am learning how to forgive
and learning how to know
when it's the right time to let go.
I am realising
that I need to forgive myself too,
for all the things I can't control
and the things I wasn't strong enough to do.

This year, I am learning.
I am learning how to heal,
learning how to push away
all of my worries, troubles and pain.
I am realising
that the cliché is true,
time really does heal all wounds.

This year, I am learning.
I am learning how to love,
learning how to care more
about people I didn't know before.
I am realising
just how big hearts can be
every time the world is hit with another tragedy.

This year I am learning.
I am learning how to live.

Living on Borrowed Time

Everything in life has an expiration date,
nothing lasts forever and no-one stays
but that doesn't mean that living life is hopeless,
we should grasp every opportunity tightly
with both hands
because for as long as we have
air to breathe and a heart that beats
there is always something wonderful to see.
I know it may seem pointless,
I know that we're living on borrowed time
but everyone has something
that they love about their life;
so, when you think of quitting while you're ahead
think of everything
that you'd never get the chance to do again.
Dry your eyes and call a friend,
remind yourself that this doesn't have to be the end.

Single

People keep telling me
that I'll find someone else,
I don't think they understand
that I'm happy by myself.
Sure, it's nice to have someone to hold
and sometimes I get a bit lonely
but I've always been comfortable with my own company.

I want to live in a world
where it's not sad to be single
because not being in a relationship
doesn't mean that I want to mingle.

Apparently, there's someone for everyone
in this place
but what if I am my own soulmate?
What if the reason I haven't found 'the one'
is because that person was me all along?
I'm the most important person in my life
and I don't need anyone else
to help me sleep at night.

The Life I Choose to Live

When you tell people that you never want
the same things they feel compelled to get
why do they always say,
"Well, you might change your mind"
and why do they say it
with so much hope in their voice?
Like I'm a lost cause who just needs to have
the same life as everyone else
for mine to matter at all.

When will people ever learn
that there's so much more to experience in this world
than everything that we've been
conditioned to believe we need?
As if life is a checklist that isn't complete
until you've ticked off marriage, a house and kids,
how boring a life must be
that only contains these three things.

So, I'm dancing to the beat of my own drum
because what's the point of living
if you're not having fun?
I'm doing what I want
and no-one can tell me that I can't.
When will people see that the only person
who can tell me how to live my life, is me?

Cinematic

I'm starting to treat my life like a movie
in which I am the protagonist,
doing whatever might make me happy
and allowing myself to feel things.
I'm starting to be brave,
to push myself to experience everything,
especially things that make me feel afraid.
Because if they don't work out the way I'd hoped
at least there will be a story to be told,
a profound message to unfold before the final credits roll.
I don't want to hide behind the curtain
and be a secondary character anymore,
to just be the friend of the person who is loved more.
I want to give myself the chance
to be a person I would admire
and I know that it won't be automatic
but I want my life to feel cinematic.

A Rare Occurrence

Falling asleep and waking up
happy
is a rare occurrence
but one I've experienced more often
since leaving you.

Butterflies

These butterflies that you placed in my stomach
escaped a long time ago
but I was too afraid to tell you
because I didn't know exactly
when and where they'd gone.
I guess they finally had enough
of being cooped up for so long,
of never being able to use
the wings that they'd always dreamt of.

For the past few years
I was cocooned inside my own mind,
waiting for the day that I was ready to say goodbye.
Flying out of my chrysalis,
I'm free to go wherever I want,
now that you're no longer
something I have to think of.

Life is a Multitude of Choices

I've figured out that life is just a multitude of choices and right or wrong, they all have consequences. Like a really long and complicated game of Snakes and Ladders; make the right choice and you'll go forward in life but the wrong one could send you falling down. But that's okay because we have the capability to do anything that our heart desires, so it's never too late to climb back up that ladder again. It's never too late to learn from our mistakes and to guide our lives towards better days.

Remember How to Breathe

When the world feels like it's attacking you,
keep your head held high
and your armour by your side.
Fight the pain head-on
and remember all the other times
when you were able to stay strong.

When you cry so many tears
that they could fill an ocean,
remember the times you laughed so much
that you forgot everything that was hurting.

When life gets to be too much,
remember how to breathe,
in, out, then repeat.
Take all the time that you need
because time is on your side
for as long as you stay alive.

Clarity

I can't stop tossing and turning at night
because there are too many thoughts
running through my mind
but this thrills me because I feel so alive.
My fingers itch to write the words down;
my brain takes over and goes to town.
Suddenly, it's 2 AM
and I've had no sleep
but I do now have a new sense of clarity
that led me to
a deeper understanding of life
and where mine is taking me.

Scavenger

I am a scavenger of words,
I collect them all,
especially the ones that make me feel.
I search for them high and low;
from music and books
to graffiti on a building wall.
I am fascinated by the way
they can weave a tale
and make the world make more sense,
how they can take my breath away
and put my heart back together again.

I am in love with the way
some words have made me feel less alone
and so, for that reason, I write my own
in the hope that someone
will read the words that I've penned
and know, that even though we have never met,
I'll always be their friend.

Living the Ordinary Life

I don't need to become famous
or make my name known,
I just need to die knowing
that I made at least
one person's life worthwhile.

I don't need to make lots of money,
to buy fancy houses and cars
I just need to do something I love
and stay true to who I am.

I don't need to travel the world
or see the seven wonders,
I don't need to check things off a bucket list
to turn my life into an adventure.

No, I don't need to accomplish a lot in life,
I just need to make it mine.
Just as long as I end up happy,
I'm perfectly fine with being ordinary.

The Story of Us

I don't think that I was ever in love with you
but I'll never forget what it felt like
to believe that I was.
Before there was an us
I'd never had a you in my life,
had never met anyone
I would eventually call mine.
So, I conjured up an idea of you in my head,
the perfect image of the perfect boyfriend
but life doesn't play out
like the movies I've seen and the books I've read
so, you never followed the script.
I think I realised early on that you weren't right for me
but I was still caught up in your love
and I turned my fantasy story into a series.
Then I guess you just became a part of the furniture,
a part of my routine that I couldn't break
and I guess I thought that I owed you something
because I used to believe that it was you
who made me the person I am today.
I found you, before I found myself
and I made the rookie mistake
of placing my love and happiness
into the hands of someone else.
But I realised that I couldn't carry on living
this life with you,
every day giving me the feeling of déjà vu
and now that it's finally come to an end
I won't be writing the story of us again.

Be Kind to Yourself

We are our own worst enemy,
there is nothing anyone could call us
that we haven't thought about already.
No-one can hurt us
quite as much as we hurt ourselves
and no-one can bring us down
if we're already living in hell.

But we don't deserve anything
that we put ourselves through
because, you see
none of those terrible thoughts
are actually true.
We all want to be treated
the same way we treat everyone else,
so why don't we start being kind to ourselves?

Reading Old Poems

I've been reading my old poems
and it's painful re-visiting memories
of how I used to feel about you,
like you were the person
who put the stars in the sky,
the person who made me
glad to be alive.
Because I've realised now
that believing I was in love with you
was just a delusion,
a make-believe story
to keep up the illusion
that you were the reason why
I wanted to make something of my life.

It's All Uphill from Here

I used to be afraid of not knowing
exactly where my life was headed
but now I take comfort in the fact
that this is not as good as it gets.
I'm confident that my life
is only going to get better
than it already is
and I can't wait to see
what else the world has in store for me.

We Are Going to Die

Eventually, we are going to die,
it's the only thing that's guaranteed in life.
So why are we so afraid of living?
Why are we so afraid of being who we really are
or doing what we want to do?
Because, one day,
everything you know will be taken away
so, don't leave it too late to realise
that you have done nothing with your life.
Write that book you've always wanted to write,
travel to that country you've always wanted to see,
become the person that you used to tell yourself
you were one day going to be.
Do not let the fear of dying
stop you from doing something with your life now.
Because despite how careful you are
and how healthy you try to be,
the only thing in life that's guaranteed
is that it doesn't last forever
and we could die at any moment
whether we want to accept it or not.
As much as I want to believe
that there's more to life than this,
that at the end, we're going to be rewarded,
as far as I know, this is the only one we get.
So, take it.
This is your life, so live it.

Letting Go of Us

I held on to you for as long as I could
but the rope became even more frayed
with every tear that I withstood.
The years passed by, each one quicker than the last
and each January I fooled myself
that this year would be our best,
the one where our future would start to take shape,
the future I'd spent so long trying to create.
But there comes a point in everyone's life
where you just have to let go
of everything that is weighing you down
and people that you used to know.
I guess I was scared of the unknown
because it had been so long since I was on my own.
If only I'd remembered
how much I used to love being by myself
before I believed
that your happiness came before anything else,
then maybe I would have learnt my lesson
a long time ago,
that a leopard never changes its spots
and our relationship was never going to be
something that it was not.

Hurdles

Sometimes, you have to take a step back in life
to get to where you need to be
because it's impossible to get everything right
on the first try
and as long as you realise that you can do better,
it's never too late to get your life together.
I used to feel like I was lagging behind,
like my life was an hourglass
and I was running out of time
but some people stay in the same place
for the rest of their days
so now I think that I'm doing okay.
I know that my life has not yet ran its course,
so, I'm excited for everything that's yet to come.
I'm looking forward to the next set of hurdles
that I'll have to jump.

Narrator

It's a freeing feeling
when you take control of your destiny,
when you become the narrator
of your own story.
I used to sit around waiting
for change to knock on my door
until I realised that it's me
I was really waiting for.

Apologies

I am the first to apologise
when I've done something wrong,
when I've realised that I wasn't right
about something, all along.
I know when I've hurt people
and immediately say sorry
but for the longest time,
I never felt like I should
apologise to me,
for the times when I looked in the mirror
and couldn't see anything to love,
for the times when I felt like
I would never be good enough.
Flaws are what make us beautiful,
this I'm now starting to see
and I'll never apologise to anyone
for the times when I'm just being me.

I Want to Be Good

I want to be the reason why
someone smiles today,
even if only for a second
before their troubles get in the way.
Because I remember a time in my life
when I had nothing to smile about,
I remember a time
when nothing felt right.

I know that this place
is rid with suffering and hurt
but I want to be the good
that people believe is still in the world.
Sometimes all it takes
is one small act of kindness
to brighten up someone's life
and make them believe that everything
will be alright.

New Years, Old Habits

Every year, we make resolutions
every year, we forget to keep them.
We think we're boring without alcohol,
the gym is too tiring;
I wonder what would happen
if we tried something we actually believed in.
Like writing that book you've been wanting to
since you were twelve
or boarding a plane
and travelling around the world.
I wonder what would happen
if we made resolutions in July
because what is New Year's Day
other than a reminder
that life is passing us by?
Yes, life is passing by
and I don't mean to shock you
but someday, you won't see
another New Year's Day.
So, do what you want right now,
while you still can,
instead of waiting for New Year's
to come back around.

On the Outside, Looking In

People always ask me
"How are you so wise for someone so young?"
and the truth is,
I grew up on the outside, looking in,
I watched how other people lived their lives
which helped me to understand the world better
and, in retrospect,
taught me how not to live mine.
I've figured out
that you get to know the difference
between right and wrong
and good and evil
by seeing, rather than doing
because you get to see the consequences
that each wrong decision brings.
I have learnt that people
really aren't as different as you think,
we all share the same manners, thoughts and feelings
and I've realised that the world
is not as perfect as some people pretend it is.
But I've also noticed
that there are others who have seen this,
because, like me, they too
have stopped every so often
to take a look at the world
and realise what is happening.
They too have noticed the hatred,
the wars, the corruption,
the segregation and the destruction.
They too have concluded
that this is not how the world should be.
We shouldn't be turning a blind eye
to the horrors of the world, but rather,

helping others in their time of need
and realising that we should all be united.

The Best Person

I used to believe
that I wanted to be someone else
until I realised that
the best person I could possibly be
is myself.

Jigsaw Puzzle

I love how some things can bring back certain memories-
like that song you played for me
that ended up being ours
or how seeing five pence reminds me
of when we lay in my back garden,
staring at the stars.
It's like having a scrapbook inside your mind,
each memento that you stumble upon,
transporting you back to that moment in time.
It could be anything from a smell to a sound,
memories that you thought were lost
can always be found
and it fascinates me how the mind works this way,
how it can conjure up a flashback
even if it's been so long
since everything changed.
Because I haven't seen you in what feels like forever
but I still so vividly remember
everything that happened when we were together
and I no longer feel sad
that we couldn't make our love last,
I no longer feel like I wasted all the time that we had
because everything that happens in life,
every memory that gets stored,
makes up the person I am
and the person I'll become.
It's like a jigsaw puzzle that you've undertook,
it takes a while to put together
and sometimes the pieces don't fit
where you think they should
but eventually, the puzzle will be finished
and the precious time spent will absolutely be worth it.
I'm looking forward to building the jigsaw of my life,

to placing the last piece in that empty space
and knowing that I finally got it right.

Everyone Needs Someone

I've heard people say before
that everyone needs someone
and while I think that's true,
'someone' doesn't have to be
a person who falls in love with you.
We have normalised the notion
that everyone must fall in love
and settle down,
that no-one could possibly be happy
until a lover has been found.
But that someone could be
a best friend you always can't wait to see,
it could be a celebrity you've never even met,
but you feel like they understand you
better than anyone else.
And call me crazy but what if
the only person you ever really **need**
is yourself?

Bloom

To my past self,
hang in there.
Your life does get better,
I swear.
I know that right now,
there's a dark cloud
hanging over your head
and it feels like
you'll never see sunlight again.
But flowers need a little rain
to help them bloom
and that's exactly
what you're going to do.

Would I Still Be Proud of Me?

If the old version of me
could see me now,
would she be proud and happy
with the choices that I made for us?
Would she understand why
people who we used to love
are no longer in our lives?
Would she realise that everything
eventually turned out alright?

If I could see
the future version of me,
would I still
be in love with my life
and eager to greet every day
with a smile?
Would I see that I'd accomplished
everything that I'd hoped to achieve?
Would I still be proud of me?

The Woman I Am Today

I don't think I'm affected by things
as much as I used to be
but I still sometimes feel like
that scared little girl
who took everything people said to her personally.
It's easy to get lost inside your own head,
to analyze and twist every little thing said.
It's easy to direct a scene
and fantasize about how life could have been
and I still sometimes feel like that scared little girl
alone and hiding in the shadows of the world.
It's easy to convince yourself that you're alone in life
when you haven't got anyone to hold at night,
it's easy to believe that you need to change to be loved
when just being yourself is always enough.
So, I must remind myself of the woman I am today;
beautiful, brilliant and brave.
I must remind myself of all that I'm going to be
and I can't wait until I can say
that it was easy.

Acknowledgments

To Stephanie Forrest, thank you for all your ideas and advice for this book and for being my number one fan of much more than just my poems.

To Kasia Wronska, thank you for being my best friend, for letting me play a part in the story of your life and for being part of the reason why I'm no longer 'the girl I used to be.'

To David Jee, thank you for your help and constructive criticism with both this book and 'In the Spaces Between the Shadows.' Also, thank you for just being a good friend.

To Will Slater, thank you for keeping me entertained during the lock-down and for letting me mither you to death with ideas for the book cover... and for saying that I wasn't mithering you.

Thank you to my followers and everyone else who has read my poems and enjoyed them. Without your support and kind words, I wouldn't have had enough confidence to publish these poems.

About the Author

Laura Harrison is a poet living in Manchester, England with her parents and dogs.
She started writing in 2012 in an attempt to make sense of the world and her feelings.
When she isn't writing, she can always be found listening to music or with her nose stuck in the pages of a good novel.
'The Moments That Freed Me' is her second collection of poetry following 'In the Spaces Between the Shadows.'

@lauraharrisonpoetry

Printed in Great Britain
by Amazon